THE FIRST CARS

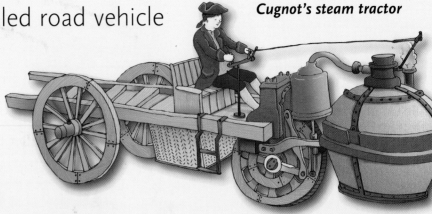

Cugnot's steam tractor

The first self-propelled road vehicle was a tractor designed to pull heavy guns. It was built by Frenchman Nicolas Cugnot in 1769. Powered by a steam engine, the machine had a top speed of 2 1/2 mph. The first real cars arrived with the invention of the internal combustion engine. German engineer Karl Benz built the first gasoline-driven car in 1885. Its rear wheels were connected to the engine by belts and chains. Early four-wheeled cars were known as "horseless carriages."

Benz 1885 car

Mercedes 35 hp

By the beginning of the 1900s, modern kinds of engines, tires, gears, and steering had all been invented. The first car to include all these features was the *Mercedes 35 hp*. Built by the German company Daimler in 1901, it was a luxury car only the rich could afford. The first inexpensive car appeared in 1908. Large numbers of the Ford Model T were built by the American Ford company in a factory.

Ford Model T ("Tin Lizzie")

TYPES OF CAR

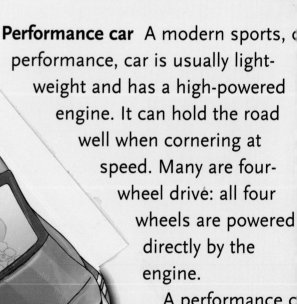

Cars are small vehicles with room for a driver and a few passengers. Sedan cars have a separate trunk, hatchbacks have room for luggage behind the back seat, while station wagons have a larger space for carrying extra loads. Some cars are specially designed for speed, including racing (see page 12).

This is a modern performance car. The engine, the same as a type used in light aircraft, is mounted at the rear of the car rather than at the front.

Performance car A modern sports, or performance, car is usually light-weight and has a high-powered engine. It can hold the road well when cornering at speed. Many are four-wheel drive: all four wheels are powered directly by the engine.

A performance car is often fitted with a turbocharged engine: air is pumped into the engine to boost its power.

A modern car is powered by an internal combustion engine fueled by gasoline or diesel fuel *(see page 8)*. The engine is usually at the front of the car, mounted at right angles to the direction in which the car travels. The driver can make the car go faster by pressing the gas pedal, which increases the power from the engine. The car slows down when the brake pedal is pressed.

Modern cars are fitted with seatbelts, side-impact bars, and air bags to protect passengers if they crash. Anti-lock brakes reduce the risk of skidding.

Electric car An alternative to a car fueled by gasoline or diesel fuel is an electric car. Instead of an internal combustion engine, the car is fitted with batteries that power an electric motor. The car is "refueled" by recharging its batteries. While electric cars give off less pollution, they use up more electricity produced by power stations.

This is a typical EV (Electric Vehicle). Some owners recharge the batteries using rooftop solar panels.

5

PARTS OF A CAR

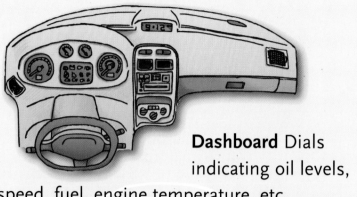

Dashboard Dials indicating oil levels, speed, fuel, engine temperature, etc., together with controls for wiper blades, headlights, heating, and radio, are all found on the car dashboard.

Pedals From the left, these are: the clutch, which the driver presses down when changing gear, brake pedal, and gas pedal.

Parking brake This lever operates the rear brakes mechanically.

Gear stick This allows the driver to choose the right gear.

Engine The car's wheels are driven by a piston engine. The engine is lubricated by oil pumped around its moving parts.

Exhaust A pipe takes exhaust fumes away from the engine and out at the rear of the car. The exhaust pipe leads to a catalytic converter, which clears emissions, and a muffler, which reduces the noise of the exhaust.

Fuel tank This holds the fuel, usually gasoline or diesel fuel, for the engine.

Suspension The suspension allows the car to drive smoothly over a bumpy road. A coil spring and a shock absorber are attached to each wheel. The springs take the force of the jolts, while the shock absorbers dampen the up and down movement of the springs, giving a smooth ride.

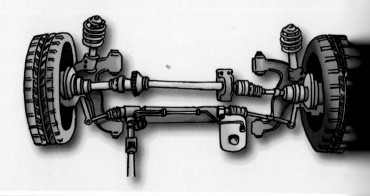

Radiator A pump drives water around channels inside the engine to cool it. The hot water then passes to the radiator, where heat is lost to the air.

Coolant reservoir The water that cools the engine is mixed with antifreeze to stop it freezing in cold weather.

Battery A car battery produces the strong current needed to turn the starter motor. It contains plates of lead immersed in acid.

PARTS OF AN ENGINE

Spark plug

The spark plugs ignite the fuel/air mixture inside the cylinders.

Valve The inlet valve lets in the fuel/air mixture; the exhaust valve lets out the exhaust gases.

Oil cap

Lubricating oil allows the engine's moving parts to slide alongside one another smoothly.

Piston The up-and-down movement of the pistons is turned into a circular motion by the crankshaft.

Crankshaft
Besides turning the whee of the car, the crankshaft also drives the fanbelt, powers the alternator, and turns the camshaft.

Oil filter
Oil passing through the filter is cleaned of dirt or grit.

Camshaft The camshaft opens and closes the valves.

Drive belt
Taking power from the crank-shaft, this drive the alternator.

Fuel injector This injects a fine spray of fuel into each cylinder.

Header
Exhaust fumes escape the cylinders via the exhaust valve, and are piped out of the engine through the header.

Dipstick This is used to check the level of oil in the engine.

Timing belt The camshaft is turned by the crank-shaft. It is connected to it by this timing belt.

Fan Driven by a small electric motor, the fan helps to keep the engine cool.

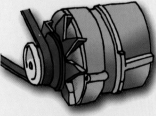
Alternator Powered b the crankshaft, this produces electrical power for the car.

A car is powered by a piston engine. It is a kind of internal combustion engine, so called because fuel, usually either gasoline or diesel, is burned (combusted) inside it. Fuel is pumped from the tank to an electronic fuel-injection system. There it is turned into a fine spray and mixed with air. Inlet valves let the fuel/air mixture into the engine's cylinders, where it is ignited by electric spark plugs. The resulting explosions drive the pistons inside the cylinders down. The crankshaft turns this up-and-down motion into a turning motion.

MOVING FORWARD

A car engine relies on pistons for its power. They move up and down very quickly inside their cylinders, turning the crankshaft. The crankshaft is connected to the wheels by gears. The wheels are made to turn around, and so the car moves forward (or backward when the car is in reverse gear). The driver controls the car using the gas pedal, which adjusts the car's speed, brake pedal, clutch, steering wheel, and gear stick.

THE FOUR-STROKE CYCLE

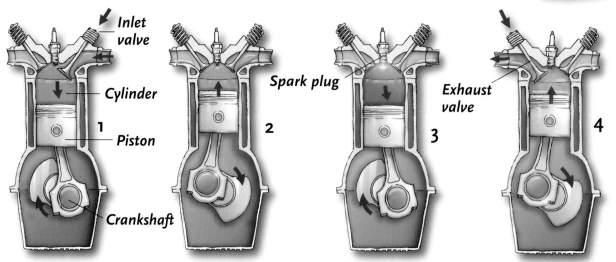

Inlet valve

Cylinder

Spark plug

Exhaust valve

Piston

1   2   3   4

Crankshaft

On the first stroke (1), the piston moves down and the inlet valve opens. A mixture of fuel and air is sucked into the cylinder. The fuel/air mixture is squeezed when the piston completes its second stroke (2). At that moment, a spark ignites it.

The explosion forces the piston down again: the third stroke (3). As the piston rises on the fourth stroke (4), the exhaust valve opens to let out the waste gases. The four-stroke cycle is repeated again and again as the pistons move up and down.

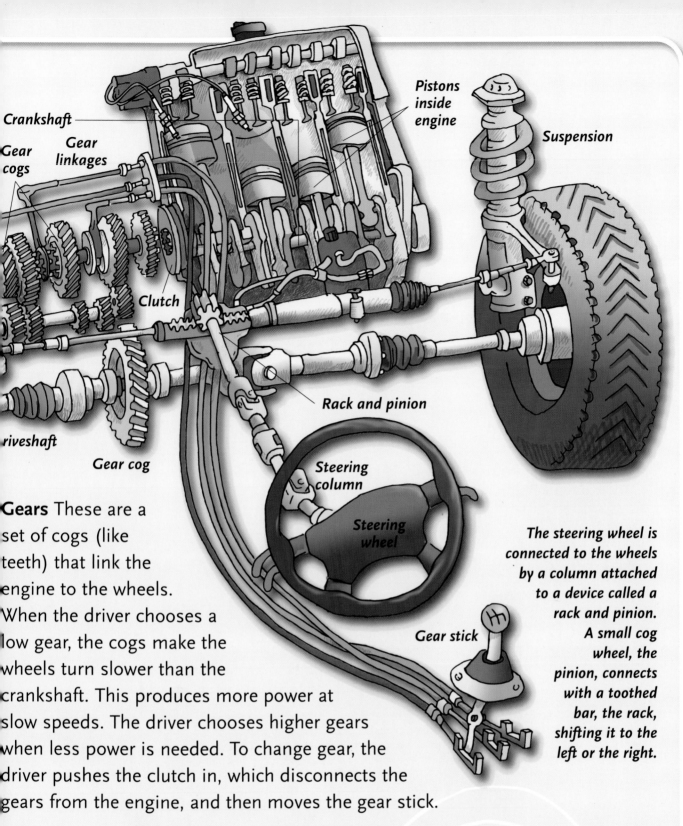

Crankshaft

Pistons inside engine

Suspension

Gear cogs

Gear linkages

Clutch

Rack and pinion

Driveshaft

Gear cog

Steering column

Steering wheel

Gear stick

Gears These are a set of cogs (like teeth) that link the engine to the wheels. When the driver chooses a low gear, the cogs make the wheels turn slower than the crankshaft. This produces more power at slow speeds. The driver chooses higher gears when less power is needed. To change gear, the driver pushes the clutch in, which disconnects the gears from the engine, and then moves the gear stick.

The steering wheel is connected to the wheels by a column attached to a device called a rack and pinion. A small cog wheel, the pinion, connects with a toothed bar, the rack, shifting it to the left or the right.

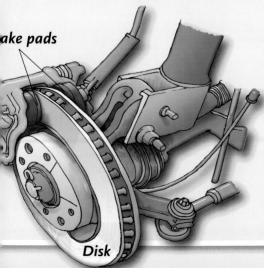

Brake pads

Disk

Brakes When the driver pushes the brake pedal, two brake pads grip a disk fitted to the inside of each of the car's wheels. These slow the wheels down. The brake pedal is linked to a hydraulic braking system. The force of the driver's foot increases pressure on fluid inside the wheel cylinders. This, in turn, forces pistons to push the brake pads against the disk.

FORMULA 1 RACING CAR

Formula 1 is an annual competition in which drivers race on different circuits around the world. The cars they drive use the latest technology to maximize speed, reliability, and safety. A modern race team involves a large number of engineers, technical experts, and pit-lane mechanics, as well as the driver.

A Formula 1 car's brakes must work at temperatures of 1800°F without parts melting. The car slows from 60 to 0 mph in only about 60 feet, compared with just over 90 feet in a performance car (see page 4).

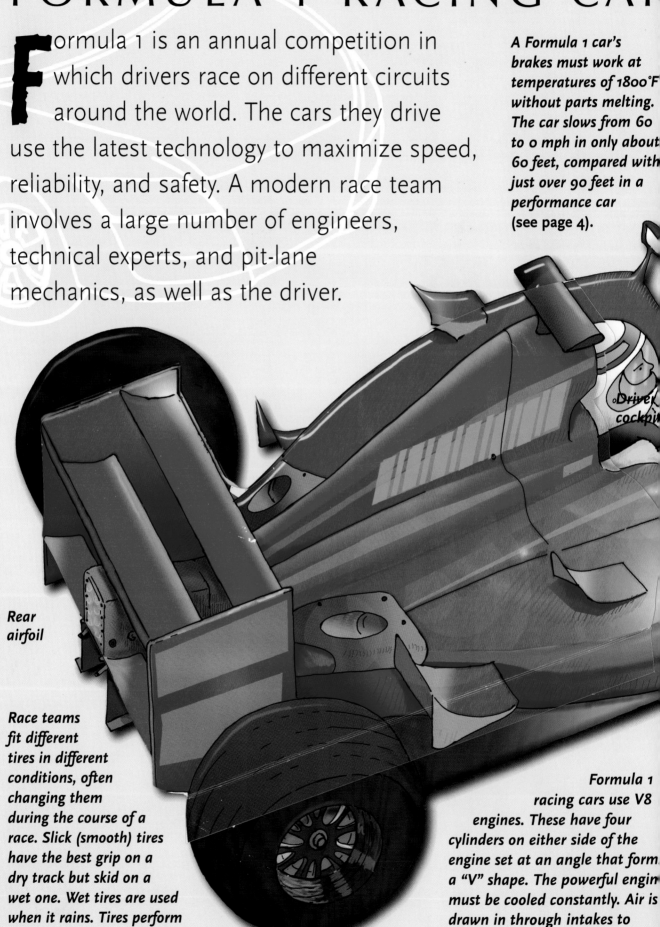

Rear airfoil

Driver cockpit

Race teams fit different tires in different conditions, often changing them during the course of a race. Slick (smooth) tires have the best grip on a dry track but skid on a wet one. Wet tires are used when it rains. Tires perform best at high temperatures.

Formula 1 racing cars use V8 engines. These have four cylinders on either side of the engine set at an angle that form a "V" shape. The powerful engine must be cooled constantly. Air is drawn in through intakes to supply cooling air to the radiator.

At high speed, the air itself holds back the most powerful vehicle, so a Formula 1 car has a smooth, streamlined shape to keep this air resistance to a minimum.

The car must weigh as little as possible. Its shell, called a single-piece monocoque, is made of an extremely light carbon fiber material. Front and rear airfoils, together with "wings" to the left and right of the cockpit, create a force that presses the car down onto the road. This improves the grip of the tires.

Front airfoil

Tire

Wing

The suspension and steering struts have a curved, streamlined shape. This helps to reduce air resistance.

GREAT RACERS

Motor racing began in 1894. The events became known as Grand Prix races. The cars' weight was limited by an agreed "formula." The German Silver Arrows, so called because they were left unpainted to reduce weight, dominated Grand Prix racing in the 1930s.

The German-built Mercedes Benz W125 was the most powerful racing car of its day. It reached speeds of more than 185 mph in 1937.

AT THE WHEEL

The steering wheel of a Formula 1 car is not like an ordinary car wheel. The controls, a set of buttons, switches, and toggles (easy-to-grab switches), are positioned on the wheel itself so the driver's hands do not have to move far from the grip.

Clutch and gears On a normal car, the clutch is a pedal and the gears are changed using a stick (see page 11). Here, the clutch and gears are controlled by hand. They are "paddles" fixed to the back of the steering wheel.

Neutral (1) This button selects neutral gear. The engine is still running but, because it is disconnected from the wheels, the car stands still.

Pit lane speed limiter (2) This prevents the car from going too fast in the pit lane.

Cockpit lights (3) The warning flags used in the race—blue, red, and yellow—also appear as lights on the wheel.

Display scroll: down

Clutch paddle

Engine stop

Main display

Gear shift: down

Oil pump

Tire pressure switch